Quips & Quotes

for preachers, teachers, speakers and editors

Collected by **H. J. Richards**

First published in 1997 by
KEVIN MAYHEW LTD
Rattlesden
Bury St Edmunds
Suffolk IP30 0SZ

0 1 2 3 4 5 6 7 8 9

ISBN 1 84003 094 1
Catalogue No 1500152

Cover design by Jaquetta Sergeant
Typesetting by Louise Hill
Printed and bound in Great Britain

FOREWORD

In my last year at school, our sixth-form teacher told us that it was the mark of an educated person to keep a Commonplace Book in which to record the memorable things one had heard or read, thus forming one's own personal anthology. Being a model student, I followed this advice religiously, and a row of exercise books on my bookshelves bears witness to my many years of fruitful squirreling.

In this book I hope to share some of my hoard, knowing that preachers, teachers, public speakers and magazine editors will find here (as I have done) wit and wisdom, asides and *bons mots*, humour and earthy common sense to suit all tastes. I have not tried to reduce the marvellous miscellany into any order, but have simply provided an extensive index to help locate the entries.

G. K. Chesterton once offered an explanation of what Jesus was up to on the numerous occasions when he is said to have left his disciples and gone off into the hills on his own. He suggested that Jesus simply had to get away from time to time to laugh his head off over the absurd things we do and say, especially in the name of religion. There are plenty of such examples in this collection, well balanced (I hope) by the many profound epigrams into which wise people through the ages have compressed their insights. Enjoy.

H. J. RICHARDS

1

A pessimist is simply an optimist who is better informed.

2

The captain of a ship sees a bright light converging on him in the dark and sends out a message: 'You had better alter course; I am a destroyer.' He receives a message in return: 'You had better alter course: I am a lighthouse.'

3

There is no such thing as a little garlic.

A. Baer

4

The humble, the gentle, the merciful, the just, the devout and loyal souls all belong to one religion: and when death takes away the masks, they will recognise each other, even though the different uniforms they wear here make them look like strangers.

William Penn (1644-1718)

5

Why can't people accept me at my mask value?

6

If I tell you who I am, you may not like who I am, and it's all I've got.

7

One is not half of two; two are halves of one.

8

When you build a wall, check what you're walling in as well as what you're walling out.

9

The study of Canon Law sharpens the mind by narrowing it.

10

Among the animals Noah took on board the Ark, did he include woodworms?

11

Fools rush in and get the best seats.

12

My brother doesn't need a keeper: he needs a brother.

Colin Morris

13

When people ask whether there is any proof that there is a life after death, I tell them about the House of Lords.

Jeremy Thorpe (b. 1929)

14

Some hae meat, and canna eat, and some wad eat that want it. But we hae meat and we can eat, and sae the Lord be thankit.

Robert Burns (1759-1796)

15

The optimist says we live in the best of all possible worlds.
The pessimist is afraid that this may be true.

16

Perhaps it is better for the world if one has a broken heart:
one is quick to recognise it elsewhere.

Helen Waddell (1889-1965)

17

The course of a river is almost always disapproved of by
its source.

Jean Cocteau (1889-1963)

18

Those who are not busy being born are busy dying.

19

When St Peter opens the Golden Gates to let us in, he will
give us the choice of two doors to go through. One has a
notice saying 'Heaven', and the other 'Discussion on
Heaven'.

20

Serve the Lord. The pay isn't much, but the retirement
benefits are out of this world.

21

Last night, Lord, I dreamed *I* made a world, and put you in it.

Peter De Rosa (b. 1932)

22

Dear God, if you're thinking of providing for me today like you did yesterday, forget it.

Peter De Rosa (b. 1932)

23

Life is like playing a violin solo in public, and learning the instrument as one goes on.

Samuel Butler (1835-1902)

24

Only our concept of time makes it possible for us to speak of the Day of Judgement by that name. In reality it is a summary court in perpetual session.

Franz Kafka (1883-1924)

25

If the rich could hire other people to die for them, the poor could make a wonderful living.

Yiddish proverb

26

Dreaming permits each and every one of us to be quietly and safely insane every night of our lives.

Charles Fisher

27

The Chinese word for 'crisis' is spelt with two ideograms: one means 'risk' and the other 'opportunity'.

28

Those who love in the Lord never see each other for the last time.

German proverb

29

God forgives sins, otherwise heaven would be empty.

30

If all mankind minus one were of one opinion, mankind would be no more justified in silencing that one person than he, if he had the power, would be justified in silencing mankind.

John Stuart Mill (1806-1873)

31

A three-day warning is given of the arrival of a tidal wave. The Catholic priest tells his flock to confess their sins and pray for forgiveness.

The Protestant pastor tells his congregation to seek out those whom they have wronged and make amends.

The Jewish rabbi tells his people that they have just three days to learn to live under water.

32

Mud thrown is ground lost.

33

The old think that the world will end when they die.
The young think it began when they were born.

Cardinal Suenens (b. 1904)

34

In a dispute about the boundary dividing Heaven from Hell,
God and Satan were unable to come to an agreement, and
referred the matter to their lawyers. Satan left the meeting
laughing, asking, 'Where is *he* going to find a lawyer?'

35

He thinks he's a wit. Well, he's half right.

36

Gandhi, asked what he thought of western civilisation,
replied, 'I think it would be a good idea.'

37

Dogma anaesthetises the mind against the agony of first-
hand experience of the truth it expresses.

Monica Furlong

38

Dogma advises us not to have an 'unconscious'.

Carl Jung (1875-1961)

39

No greater disservice could be done to Religion in this country than that religious education in schools should be the half-hearted communication of half-comprehended truths by the half-trained to the half-interested.

A. G. Wedderspoon (1964)

40

When asked why she always bowed her head when Satan was mentioned, the woman replied, 'It costs nothing to be polite.'

41

The man who sticks to the middle of the road is sooner or later going to be knocked down.

42

I used to be indecisive, but now I'm not so sure.

43

Those whom the gods love grow young.

Oscar Wilde (1854-1900)

44

He's a strange man. When you ask him, 'How are you?', he tells you!

45

There are so many hungry people in the world that God cannot appear to them except in the form of bread.

Mahatma Gandhi (1869-1948)

46

If you were arrested as a Christian, would there be sufficient evidence to convict you?

47

A bird doesn't sing because it has an answer; it sings because it has a song.

48

Do we argue in order to win, over the other person, or in order to win-over the other person?

49

Enduring the unendurable – that's what endurance is really about.

50

He who would do good to another must do it in minute particulars.

William Blake (1757-1827)

51

A dog that dies, and that knows that it dies like a dog, and that can say that it knows that it dies like a dog – is a man.

Erich Fried

52

To say that God comes down is simply a way of saying that we are not near God.

Mahatma Gandhi (1869-1948)

53

In the world to come, they will not ask me, 'Why were you not Moses?' but, 'Why were you not Zusya?'

Rabbi Zusya of Hanipol

54

It is not enough to point one's armchair in the direction of history.

Albert Camus (1913-1960)

55

I never realised how well I was until I gave up thinking how ill I was.

St Teresa of Avila (1515-1582)

56

The depth of darkness into which you can descend, and still live, is exactly equivalent to the height you can reach if you want.

57

Man is never literal in the expression of his ideas except in matters most trivial.

Rabindranath Tagore (1861-1941)

58

Those who don't believe in miracles are not realists.
Israeli saying

59

To err is human; to er-er-er is unforgivable.

60

If you ask for the Irish equivalent of 'mañana', you will be told that there is no word in the language for conveying the same sense of urgency.

61

The pollution is getting so bad that even atheists can walk on the water.

62

'The ghost is happy but the meat is soft.'
'Invisible maniac.'
Computer translations of 'The spirit is willing but the flesh is weak' *and* 'Out of sight out of mind'.

63

Glosses on the Parable of the Good Samaritan:
The Levite could not stop because he was on the way to a Conference on Caring.
The Samaritan's first concern was to find out if the wounded man had read the Samaritan Pentateuch.
A Social Worker was worried about the man who had committed the assault: 'He needs my help.'

64

One cannot talk about God merely by talking about man in a loud voice.

Karl Barth (1886-1968)

65

Cigarette smoking can seriously damage your health.
But thanks for building Polaris.

66

One disadvantage of being a hog is that at any moment some blundering fool may try to make a silk purse out of your wife's ear.

Beachcomber (1893-1979)

67

'. . . And may the peace of Christ thoroughly disturb you.'

68

This wallpaper is killing me. One of us will have to go.

Reputed last words of Oscar Wilde (1854-1900)

69

A notice outside a convent:
Trespassers will be prosecuted with the full rigour of the law. Signed: Sisters of Mercy.

70

None of us is perfect. I myself am peculiarly susceptible to draughts.

Oscar Wilde (1854-1900)

71

Pope John Paul II is granted a vision in which he is told he may have the answer to any three questions he wishes to put. 'Will we have married priests in the Church?' 'Not in your lifetime.'
'Will women be ordained priests in the Church?' 'Not in your lifetime.'
'Will there be another Polish pope in the Church?' 'Not in my lifetime.'

72

Moishe, arriving in heaven, is shown into a waiting room, where a TV screen is showing the exotic orgies going on in hell. Anticipating something even more exciting in heaven, he is surprised when God finally appears with two tuna sandwiches. 'Is this all I'm going to get?' 'Well, for the two of us, it was hardly worth cooking.'

73

I've worked myself up from nothing to a state of extreme poverty.

Groucho Marx (1895-1977)

74

Most people are troubled by the Scripture passages they don't understand. I'm most troubled by the passages I *do* understand.

Mark Twain (1835-1910)

75

A rabbi tells his son to go and give a penny to a blind man. 'Why didn't you raise your hat to him?'
'Because he's blind.'
'How do you know he's not an impostor? Go back and raise your hat.'

76

A traveller asks for overnight shelter in Abraham's tent, and Abraham invites him to join him in prayer to the one God. The man refuses, saying he is an atheist, and Abraham drives him out. God complains: 'I have put up with that man for 70 years, and you can't put up with him for one night?'

77

I like work. It fascinates me. I can sit and look at it for hours.

Jerome K. Jerome (1859-1927)

78

God's mistake was to forbid the apple. He should have forbidden the serpent, and Adam would have eaten that. End of problem.

79

'Do you believe in baptism?'
'Believe in it? I've actually seen it done.'

80

Conscience is a little metal triangle inside your heart. When you do wrong, it spins round, and the sharp corners hurt. But if you do it often enough, the sharp corners wear off, and it doesn't hurt any more.

81

Your theology is what you *are* when talking stops and action starts.

Colin Morris

82

Tombstone inscriptions:
'I expected this, but not yet.'
'I told you I wasn't feeling well.'

83

For a permissive age, shouldn't God have given us the Ten Suggestions?

84

He who knows not, and knows not that he knows not, is foolish. Shun him.
He who knows not, and knows that he knows not, is ignorant. Teach him.
He who knows, and knows that he knows, is wise. Follow him.

85

God and other artists are always a little obscure.

Oscar Wilde (1854-1900)

86

Don't expect people to see eye to eye with you if you look down on them.

87

God wants spiritual fruits, not religious nuts.

Ella Wilcox (1850-1919)

88

People need seven years of silent enquiry to learn truth, but fourteen more to learn how to communicate it to others.

Plato (BCE 428-348)

89

Overheard at Speakers' Corner, Hyde Park:
'If you had two houses, wouldn't you give one to the poor?'
'Of course.'
'If you had two cars, wouldn't you give one to the poor?'
'Of course.'
'If you had two shirts, wouldn't you give one to the poor?'
'Hey, I've *got* two shirts.'

90

Better a bad peace than a good war.

Jewish proverb

91

'The question of ethics is paramount. For example, today I was repaid £20 that was owed to the firm, and discovered two £20 notes stuck together. Now comes the question of ethics: do I tell my partner?'

92

An edict of the emperor Gratian published in Constantinople in AD 380:
'The people ruled by us shall practise the religion which the divine Peter preached to the people of Rome . . . and shall embrace the name of Catholic Christians. All others shall be adjudged demented and insane. As heretics, their meeting places shall not be called churches. They shall be smitten first by divine vengeance, and secondly by our own retribution.'

93

The Rabbi, preparing for Yom Kippur, stands in the synagogue beating his breast and saying, 'I am nothing, I am nothing.' The Cantor, standing alongside, does the same. The cleaner, seeing them, joins in and says, 'I am nothing, I am nothing.' The Rabbi turns to the Cantor and says, 'Look who thinks he is nothing.'

94

Ten thousand people shouting out the same thing makes it false, even if it happens to be true.

Kierkegaard (1813-1855)

95

Two people are listening to the Sermon on the Mount from some distance, nearly out of earshot. One says, 'Blessed are the cheese-makers? What's so special about them?' The other replies, 'Well, I don't imagine he would want to exclude the makers of other dairy products.'

From the Monty Python 'Life of Brian'

96

From his scaffolding high up on the Sistine ceiling, Michelangelo spotted an old woman at prayer in the chapel below. To relieve the boredom, he put on a deep voice and shouted down. 'This is Jesus Christ speaking.' She shouted back, 'Shutta up, I speaking to your mother.'

97

Don't say, 'It's only a drop in the ocean.' The whole ocean is made up of drops.

Mother Teresa (1910-1997)

98

Married people, when they think of the sort of life they live, ought to blush.

St Ambrose (339-397)

99

War is what peace rots away into.

100

It is a good job St Paul's epistles did not have to be submitted to the Holy Office in Rome. He would not have met our strict requirements of clarity and unambiguity.

Attributed in the 1960s to Cardinal Ottaviani

101

No theologian may place his own personal convictions above the teaching of the Church. Unless, of course, he happens to be pope.

Peter Hebblethwaite (d. 1987)

102

From Ambrose Bierce's Devil's Dictionary (1906):
Caaba: A large stone, preserved at Mecca, presented by the archangel Gabriel to Abraham. He had asked for bread.
Distance: The only thing the rich are willing for the poor to call their own, and keep.
Edible: Good to eat and wholesome to digest, as a worm to a toad, a toad to a snake, a snake to a pig, a pig to a man, and a man to a worm.
Evangelist: The bearer of good tidings, especially such as assure us of our own salvation and the damnation of neighbours.
Meekness: Uncommon patience in planning a revenge that is worthwhile.
Positive: Mistaken at the top of one's voice.
Revelation: A famous book in which St John the Divine concealed all that he knew. The revealing is done by the commentators, who know nothing.

103

Epitaph: In the earth we here prepare a
Place to lay our little Clara.
Reginald and Mary Frazer.
PS Gabriel will raise her.

Ambrose Bierce (1842-1914)

104

So they (the Government) go on in strange paradox, decided only to be undecided, resolved to be irresolute, adamant for drift, solid for fluidity, all-powerful for impotence.

Winston Churchill (1936)

105

The schoolgirl who was told she couldn't play the part of Mary in the Nativity Play because she was Jewish.

106

My one regret in life is not being somebody else.

Woody Allen (b. 1935)

107

Of course I believe in a life of eternal bliss after death, but why talk about such a gloomy subject?

108

Ille hic est Raphael, timuit quo sospite
vinci rerum Magna Parens, et moriente mori.

Living, great Nature feared he might outvie
her works, and dying, fears herself may die.

Inscription on Raphael's tomb by Cardinal Bembo
with translation by Alexander Pope (1688-1744)

109

If anyone wrongs you, ask yourself why he did it. When you know this, you won't be surprised or angry, only sorry for him.

Marcus Aurelius (121-180)

110

Not all good things are compatible.

Isaiah Berlin (b. 1912)

111

'May you live in interesting times.'

Arab curse

112

Violence is the only way of ensuring a hearing for moderation.

William O'Brien (1852-1928)

113

The sympathy with all living things, sinful and righteous alike, which the imaginative arts awaken, is the forgiveness of sins commanded by Christ.

W. B. Yeats (1865-1939)

114

A good indication of the kind of person you are is provided by asking yourself whether people say 'Oh good' when they see you approaching, or 'Oh God'.

115

Jesus Christ believed in a church which had power only in so far as it had no power.

116

Art is a lie which makes us realise the truth.

Picasso (1881-1973)

117

Education is the gradual growth from cocksure ignorance to thoughtful uncertainty.

118

When they reach the Pearly Gates, parish priests and curates will be greeted by St Peter with, 'Come in, my sons.' But canons, archdeacons and bishops will be detained for further questioning.

119

When my house burnt down
I got an unobstructed view
of the moon at night.

Zen saying

120

When Jesus went to a football match, he enthusiastically cheered both the Catholic goal and the Protestant one. When his neighbours asked why, he explained that he was simply enjoying the game. They asked, 'Are you some sort of atheist?'

121

How odd	Not odd
of God	of God
to choose	Goyim
the Jews.	annoy him.
Anon	*Leo Rosten*

122

The word 'friend' sometimes means nothing. The word 'enemy' never.

123

A woman's guess is much more accurate than a man's certainty.

Rudyard Kipling (1865-1936)

124

The stone fell on the jar: poor jar.
The jar fell on the stone: poor jar.

125

Fighting for peace is like fornicating for chastity.

126

The Scots minister warned his congregation that, at the end, it will be no use saying, 'But Lord, we didna ken.' As he consigns them to eternal damnation, the Almighty will say, 'Well, ye ken the noo.'

127

On another occasion, when he was preaching on the 'weeping and gnashing of teeth', and a woman cried out, 'But minister, I have no teeth', he replied, 'Teeth will be provided.'

128

All the great idol-smashers have eventually been idolised.

129

A hen is only an egg's way of making another egg.

Samuel Butler (1835-1902)

130

The religions we call false were once true.

Ralph W. Emerson (1803-1882)

131

I am wandering through a vast forest at night, with only a candle to guide me. A stranger appears and tells me to blow out my candle in order to find my way more clearly. I ask him who he is, and he tells me. A theologian.

Denis Diderot (1713-1784)

132

Just as it would be absurd to try to make children's games reasonable, it would be a great folly to try to purify religions.

133

It were better to be of no church than to be bitter for any.

William Penn (1644-1718)

134

Where there are humans
you'll find flies
and Buddhas.

Kobayashi Issa (18th century)

135

When people are free to do as they please, they generally imitate each other.

136

I don't ask for others to be faultless: only that their faults don't disturb mine.

137

Occasionally Society really values itself at its proper worth: it looks up to those who care nothing about it.

Sébastien Chamfort (1741-1794)

138

Nothing will ever be attempted if all possible objections must first be overcome.

Dr Samuel Johnson (1709-1784)

139

Those in favour of the death penalty clearly have more in common with murderers than those against it.

140

Only those with no brothers dream of all men being brothers.

141

At the execution of the Czech priest John Hus, a gentle old lady was seen bringing a pile of sticks to add to the fire.

142

The most dangerous disciple is the one whose defection would destroy the whole party: in other words the best disciple.

Friedrich Nietzsche (1844-1900)

143

It is flattering some people to endure them.

Marquess of Halifax (1633-1695)

144

If you're foolish enough to be contented, don't show it. Just grumble with the rest.

Jerome K. Jerome (1859-1927)

145

Good resolutions are useless attempts to interfere with scientific laws.

Oscar Wilde (1854-1900)

146

Most perseverance is simply a form of indecision.

147

Repentance is not a fair highway to God: it is shocking and passionate. God prefers you to approach him thoughtful, not penitent.

Henry Thoreau (1817-1862)

148

When you do someone a service, you have simply obeyed the laws of your own nature. Do you want more? Are you going to pay your eyes for seeing, or feet for walking?

Marcus Aurelius (121-180)

149

We give praise or blame according to which shows what good judgement we have.

Friedrich Nietzsche (1844-1900)

150

Rogues are easier to bear than fools: they sometimes take a rest.

Alexandre Dumas fils (1824-1895)

151

The poor know things that the rich don't know.
The sick know things that the healthy don't know.
The stupid know things that the intelligent don't know.

152

He that knows little often repeats it.

Thomas Fuller (1654-1734)

153

A University is a place which brings out every human potential, including stupidity.

Anton Chekhov (1860-1904)

154

Classical music is the kind we keep thinking will turn into a tune.

155

We easily admit that others have more courage than our-selves, or strength, or experience, or skill, or beauty. But judgement?

Montaigne (1533-1592)

156

Do not seek to follow in the footsteps of the men of old;
seek what they sought.

Matsua Basho (17th century)

157

Enough is as good as a meal.

Oscar Wilde (1854-1900)

158

Don't limit a child to your own learning: he was born in
another time.

Rabbinic

159

Whoever says that the words of the Bible are one thing,
and the words of the world are another, must be regarded
as one who denies God.

Rabbi Pinhus of Koretz (18th century)

160

People think they pray to God. They're wrong. The prayer
itself is the presence of God.

Rabbi Pinhas of Koretz (18th century)

161

Some halls in heaven open only to the sound of song.

The Jewish Zohar (1290)

162

To sin against a fellow human being is worse than sinning against God, because God is everywhere and you can always find him to put things right.

The Hasidim

163

Rabbi Baer was starving. As his wife hugged her hungry child, he shouted out in protest. A voice from heaven thundered: 'You have forfeited your share in the World to Come.' The rabbi replied, 'It doesn't matter. I'm now free of the hope for reward, and can serve God as a free man.'

The Hasidim

164

If God abandoned the truth, I would hang on to truth and let God go.

Meister Eckhart (d. 1327)

165

The real slavery of Israel in Egypt was that they had grown to tolerate it.

Rabbi Hanokh (19th century)

166

The rose that with your earthly eyes you see
Has flowered in God from all eternity.

Angelus Silesius (17th century)

167

If someone comes to you and asks for help,
don't turn him away with pious words,
'Have faith, God will help you.'
You must act as if there were no God,
as if there were only one who could help this person: you.

Rabbi Moshe Leib (19th century)

168

We have just enough religion to make us hate, but not
enough to make us love one another.

Jonathan Swift (1667-1745)

169

Apparently no one had warned John F Kennedy that in
Berlin a 'Berliner' is what you ask for when you want a
jam doughnut. Hence the wild scenes when he proudly
proclaimed, 'Ich bin ein Berliner.'

170

On the 500th anniversary of Luther's birth (1483), Pope
John Paul II proudly proclaimed the progress of ecu-
menism: 'We seem to sight from afar the dawn of the
advent of a restoration of unity.'

171

I hit you first
because I thought you were going to hit me first
because you thought I was going to hit you first.

172

If we take an eye for an eye, soon the whole world will be blind.

Mahatma Gandhi (1869-1948)

173

The Church exists not only to comfort the disturbed, but to disturb the comfortable.

174

To admit acrimony in theological discussion is itself more fundamentally heretical than any erroneous opinions upheld or condemned in the course of the discussion.

William Temple (1881-1944)

175

A child does a drawing of God. The parents say, 'But no one knows what he looks like.' The child replies, 'Well they will now.' The parents fall about laughing. But has the child said anything different from John's Gospel: 'God no one has ever seen, but the only Son has revealed him . . . he who has seen him has seen the Father'?

176

Here lies the body of W. W.
Who never more will trouble you, trouble you.

177

I have seen flowers come in stony places,
And kind things done by men with ugly faces,
And the gold cup won by the worst horse at the races.
So I trust too.

John Masefield (1878-1967)

178

When W. C. Fields was asked what he was doing browsing through a Bible on his deathbed in 1946, he said, 'Looking for loopholes.'

179

Only a mediocre person is always at his best.

Somerset Maugham (1874-1965)

180

Progress may have been all right once, but it's gone on too long.

Ogden Nash (1902-1971)

181

'Is there any place to eat in this part of Ireland?'
'Yes, there are two.'
'Which one do you advise?'
'Well, if you go to one, you'll wish you'd gone to the other.'

182

I've had a wonderful evening. This wasn't it.

Groucho Marx (1895-1977)

183
'Golders Green 2 miles. But to you, 1½'.

184
Jesus asked the beggar whether he had been blind all his life. He replied, 'Not yet.'

185
Jesus saved the world? What was it like before?

Peter De Rosa (b. 1932)

186
It is easier for a camel to pass through the eye of a needle if it is slightly greased.

Kehlog Albran

187
Not only is there no God, but try getting a plumber on a Sunday.

Woody Allen (b. 1935)

188
Whoever you are
And wherever you come from
Welcome
I am Cyrus
I won for the Persians their Empire
Do not begrudge me this little earth
Which covers my body

Inscription on tomb of Cyrus (d. BCE 529)

189

He has sat on the fence so long that the iron has entered his soul.

Lloyd George (1863-1945) on Sir John Simon

190

'It is essential that we acknowledge the equality of all the people of God, from the bishop down.'

From a bishop's pastoral letter

191

After lecturing on Jesus to a mixed group of Christians, Muslims and Hindus, a missionary was told by a venerable Hindu, 'Sir, I thank you. I have known him all my life. Now you have told me his name.'

192

When I point to the moon, stop looking at my finger.

Zen saying

193

Someone asked Karl Barth (1886-1968) whether we will see our loved ones in heaven. Barth replied, 'You'd better be prepared – not *only* your loved ones.'

194

The Church has usually been happy to be the world's icing sugar, somewhat sweetening the intolerable, but changing nothing. . . . Called by the Lord to be in the world but not of it, the Church has more often than not been of the world but not in it.

Paul Oestreicher (1987)

195

God must have loved the poor: he made so many of them.

Abraham Lincoln (1809-1865)

196

Ten Commandments
Nine choirs of Angels
Eight Beatitudes
Seven Sacraments
Six Sins against the Holy Ghost
Five Notions
Four Relations
Three Persons
Two Natures
One God
No proof.

197

The Roman lions did at least have a Christian breakfast.

Professor Joad (1891-1953)

198

The nicest thing about being a mink is that you can still hang around a woman's neck even after you're dead.

Bob Hope (b. 1903)

199

He is so low that his bottom would wipe out his footprints, if he wasn't so crooked that his bottom comes first.

200

'An hour of this rain', said the Irish farmer, 'will do more good in five minutes than a month of it would do in a week at any other time.'

201

The Romans must have thought that Jesus said, 'On this baroque I will build my Church.'

202

Johann Sebastian Bach wrote 250 cantatas and fathered 22 children. He used to practise on an old spinster in the attic.

203

God asked the man what he had done with his brother, and he turned white with fear.

204

The psychiatrist said, 'No, there's no question of any complex; you simply are inferior.'

205

Carry your cross, don't just drag it along behind you.

206

Everybody likes to see a broad smile, especially when the broad is smiling at them.

207

Forgive me for declining your invitation because of a subsequent engagement.

208

Definition of an oboe: An ill woodwind that nobody blows good.

L. McKinney

209

When someone says, 'I'll think it over and let you know', you know.

210

'Our next speaker is someone who needs all the introduction he can get.'

211

It is no good going to bed to save candles if the result is twins.

Chinese proverb

212

Exits, Are They On The Way Out?

213

In a Lebanese classroom: 'What do two and two make?' 'Am I buying or selling?'

214

From a professor's posthumous lecture notes: 'Shout here; argument weak.'

215

We should not try to unscrew the inscrutable.

216

The virtuous person is one who sticks to the straight and narrow path between right and wrong.

217

Edward VII's daughter, under Catholic instruction, was asked if she had any difficulty about the pope being head of the Church. 'Good heavens no! If my father can be head of the Church, anyone can.'

218

Pope John XXIII was asked by a visitor how many people worked in the Vatican. 'About half.'

219

The Catholic invitation to Anglicans should not be, 'We own the divine Truth; come and take it at our hands', but, 'We are unable to bear divine Truth creditably; come and help us.'

Fr Jerome's 'Catholic Plea for Reunion' (1934)

220

What we must ask ourselves is whether we are going to stay awake with the wise virgins, or go to sleep with the foolish ones.

221

Mgr Talbot, a friend of Pope Pius IX, came to preach in London shortly after the pope's death in 1878. He began by saying that he had a recent letter from the Holy Father which he proposed to read out, and asked the congregation to regard it as a voice from the unseen world. He then began to read: 'My dear Monsignor. It is very hot here . . .'

222

Life is like a sewer. What you get out of it depends on what you put in.

Tom Lehrer

223

When God wants to punish us, he answers our prayers.

224

A fanatic is someone who redoubles his effort when he has forgotten his aim.

George Santayana (1863-1952)

225

If the purpose of pornography is to excite sexual desire, it is unnecessary for the young, inconvenient for the middle-aged, and unseemly for the old.

Malcolm Muggeridge (1903-1990)

226

It very often happens that the wages of sin are birth.

227

Notice in a restaurant on the Dead Sea: 'Go easy with the salt; you don't know who it's been.'

228

It is a pity that when God limited man's intelligence, he did not also limit his stupidity.

Konrad Adenauer (1876-1967)

229

We shouldn't ask whether the Gospels hold water, when what they hold is light.

Sebastian Moore

230

Athlete's Foot is a load of rot.

231

Two psychiatrists pass each other. 'Good morning' says one. The other thinks, 'I wonder what he meant by that?'

232

His was the word that spake it,
He took the bread and brake it.
And what that word doth make it
I do believe and take it.

Attributed to Queen Elizabeth I (1533-1603)

233

The Church's perennial failing is to be so identified with the world that it cannot speak to it, or to be so remote from it that again it cannot speak to it.

John A. T. Robinson (1919-1983)

234

When Van Gogh
the brilliant mad
painter tramped through Paris
(sunflowers o sunflowers!)
after quarrelling
with Gauguin
and heard starlings
above Sacré Coeur
it went in one ear and
stayed there.

William McSweeney

235

Hearing the confessions of nuns is like being nibbled to death by ducks.

Fr Vincent McNabb

236

God so loved the world that he did not send a committee.

237

Never try to discourage thinking, for you are sure to succeed.

Bertrand Russell (1872-1970)

238

Bernard Shaw, asked to say a few words on the subject of sex, stood up and said, 'It gives me great pleasure', and sat down.

239

Do unto others before they do unto you.

240

Love your enemy: it will drive him mad.

241

'What is the first thing you must do when you go to Confession?'
'Go and commit some sins.'

242

'Will people please stand away from the bacon slicer, since we are getting a little behind with our orders.'

Radio, 'Take It From Here' (1960s)

243

I have sometimes thought of publishing the thesis that the Pharisees did not reject Christianity; on the contrary, they accepted it and joined the Church, where they were promoted to high office.

John L. McKenzie SJ

244

In a Jewish restaurant:
'Waiter, this lobster you brought me has only got one claw.'
'So maybe he was in a fight.'
'So maybe you bring me the winner.'

245

Those who do not remember the past are condemned to re-live it.

George Santayana (1863-1952)

246

Of the 36 ways of avoiding disaster, running away is the best.

Chinese proverb

247

No one gives you a black eye: you have to fight for it.

248

If you insist long enough that you're right, you'll be wrong.

249

When you face your Maker, you will have to account for all those pleasures of life that you failed to experience.

Talmud

250

From my teachers I have learnt much,
From my colleagues more,
But it was from my students
That I learnt most of all.

Rabbi Hanina (225)

251

As the heavens opened, and the Voice proclaimed, 'This is my beloved Son in whom I am well pleased', John the Baptist's eyes filled with pride, and he humbly dropped his head as he gazed and gazed into the Jordan. Apologetically Jesus tapped him on the shoulder and said, 'I think he means me.'

A. J. Llanguth

252

The problems of a nine year old cannot be solved in any way except by becoming ten.

Al Capp (1909-1979)

253

Cricket is a game which the English, not being a spiritual people, have invented to give themselves some conception of eternity.

Lord Mancroft

254

It is the dark part of the eye that sees.

Philo (1st century)

255

Dear God, I know we are your Chosen People, but couldn't you sometimes choose some other people for a change?

Sholem Aleichem (1859-1916)

256

I wouldn't join a club which would have me as a member.

Groucho Marx (1895-1977)

257

If people don't know what is impossible, they'll do it.

258

The advantage of telling the truth is that you don't have to remember what you said.

259

Graffiti:

a. Nostalgia isn't what it used to be.

b. The paranoids are after me.

c. Death is nature's way of telling you to slow down.

d. Who gives a damn about apathy?

e. Procrastinate Now.

f. I'd give my right arm to be ambidextrous.

g. Predestination was doomed to failure from the start.

h. When God made man, she was only testing.

i. I dislike graffiti.
   I dislike all Italian food.

j. Come home Oedipus, all is forgiven. Mum.
   Over my dead body. Dad.

k. *(High up)* Smoking stunts growth.
   (Low Down) Now he tells me.

l. *(High up)* Good night David.
   (Low down) Good night Goliath.

260

I am all at once what Christ is,
since he was what I am, and
this Jack, joke, poor potsherd,
patch, matchwood, immortal diamond
   is immortal diamond.

Gerard M. Hopkins (1844-1889)

261

Definitions of Jewish chutzpah (gall):

a. A fly crawling up an elephant's leg intent on rape.

b. Killing your father and mother and then throwing yourself on the mercy of the court as an orphan.

262

Every cripple has his own way of walking.

263

One way to prove you have a mind is to change it.

264

Man has places in his heart which do not yet exist, and into them suffering enters in order that they may have existence.

Léon Bloy (1846-1917)

265

He (Macaulay) has occasional flashes of silence which make his conversation quite delightful.

Sydney Smith (1771-1845)

266

Some lectures could be described in the words of the Ovaltine advert, 'Being largely pre-digested, this mixture is entirely harmless.'

Professor C. F. Evans

267

Sam Goldwynisms:

a. Include me out.

b. I'll give you a definite maybe.

c. I'll tell you in two words: Im-possible.

d. A man who goes to a psychiatrist needs his head examined.

e. This new atomic bomb – it's dynamite.

f. Since then a lot of water has been passed by all of us.

Sam Goldwyn (1882-1974)

268

That phrase ('one never knows') represented, I think, his deepest research into the meaning of life.

Grahame Greene (1904-1991)

269

One must possess a chaos within to give birth to a star.

Friedrich Nietzsche (1844-1900)

270

God cannot answer the questions which man has not yet raised.

Karl Rahner (1904-1984)

271

When he was a curate in an East End parish, John Heenan planted an acorn in the presbytery garden. Returning as Cardinal 50 years later, he was delighted to see that it had grown into a gigantic acorn.

Peter De Rosa (b. 1932)

272

Earth is here so kind,
That just tickle her with a hoe,
And she laughs with a harvest.

Douglas Jarrold (1803-1857)

273

Quotes from G. K. Chesterton (1874-1936):

a. Silence is the unbearable repartee.

b. A yawn is a silent shout.

c. I hate a quarrel because it interrupts an argument.

d. Tradition is the democracy of the dead.

e. I believe in getting into hot water. I think it keeps you clean.

274

Is your hair wavy, or does it just go in and out with your skull?

Radio, 'Take It From Here' (1960s)

275

The only things we really have are those we give up. The things we keep possess us.

Thomas Merton (1915-1968)

276

A man goes into a Soho grocery and asks for tomato sauce. 'Sorry, we have no tomato sauce in this shop, only salt.' 'Only salt? Do you ever sell any salt?' 'No. But the man I get it from, can *he* sell salt!'

277

A riot is the expression of a people who feel they have not been listened to.

Martin Luther King (1929-1968)

278

I never forget a face, but in your case I'll make an exception.

Groucho Marx (1895-1977)

279

I'll never forget what's-his-name.

280

'Have you no shame, begging like that in the open street?'
'So what do you want me to do? Open an office?'

281

To describe his acting as wooden would be unfair to trees.

282

You've got to kiss an awful lot of frogs to find a prince.

283

When I talk about the eye of God, why do you start asking
questions about eyebrows?

Ludwig Wittgenstein (1889-1951)

284

A Frenchman describes his command of English:
'You may think that of the English idiom and of the
English usage I know nothing, damn nothing. But you are
wrong. I know damn all.'

285

You can't cross a chasm in little jumps.

286

I don't believe in an after-life, but I'm taking along a
change of underwear just in case.

Woody Allen (b. 1935)

287

When the frog was created, the first words he said were, 'Lord, how you made me jump'.

Colin Morris

288

We call it a miracle if God does what we ask.
God calls it a miracle if we do what he asks.

Colin Morris

289

We complain that God seems to be a long way off. So, who moved?

Colin Morris

290

The Christian message:
If you don't love, you won't really be alive.
If you do love, and do it effectively, you'll be killed.

Herbert McCabe OP

291

In the ecumenical dialogue, we don't need to discover a new unity, but an old one. We already are one. We simply imagine we are not.

292

When the first men landed on the moon, they were over-awed to tread where no sin had ever been committed. Jewish theologians saw the event as less auspicious: these men were treading where no act of charity or compassion had ever been practised.

293

Prayer is man's attempt to communicate with the weather.

294

False religion says: Do not fear. Trust in God and he will see that none of the things you fear will happen.
True religion says: Do not fear. The things you fear may well happen to you, but they are nothing to be afraid of.

Herbert McCabe OP

295

The trouble with the Jews is that they're no better than the rest of us.

Mark Twain (1835-1910)

296

Like many other important people, God does not usually speak to us directly, but through sources close to him.

Delia Smith (b. 1947)

297

After a conference of H.M. Inspectors addressed by Margaret Thatcher:
'What did you think of her address?'
'She was immaculate, but she had no conception.'

298

You don't have to be a Catholic to know about guilt, but it certainly helps.

Bruce Kent (b. 1929)

299

Two adjacent notices in the porch of a Catholic Church:
'In this church, communion is not served in the hands.'
'Please wipe your feet.'

300

When a cannibal uses a knife and fork, you can hardly call it progress.

Geoffrey Howe (b. 1926)

301

Being attacked by Geoffrey Howe was like being savaged by a dead sheep.

Denis Healey (b. 1917)

302

King Harold to his troops at Hastings:
'There are Normans about, so keep your eyes open.'

303

Every judge, who judges a judgement of truth, true to the truth of the matter, causes the glory of God to dwell among men.

Talmud

304

It is not in stretching out your hands in prayer that you will be heard. You will be heard when you stretch out your hands to the poor.

St John Chrysostom (347-407)

305

When I give bread to the poor, they call me a saint. When I ask why the poor are poor, they call me a Communist.

Archbishop Romero (1917-1980)

306

How is it that the archbishop of Canterbury and the pope can both preach the gospel of poverty from their respective palaces, without being accused of blasphemy?

James Fenton

307

'Our Father, who art in heaven, stay there.'

308

Antisemitism is hating Jews more than is necessary.

Chief Rabbi Jacobivitz (1980)

309

F. *Mauriac opposing the unification of Germany.* 'I love Germany so much, I want to have two of them.'

François Mauriac (1885-1970)

310

All sunshine makes a desert.

Arab proverb

311

Jesus does not call people to religion, but to life.

Paul Tillich (1886-1965)

312

We would all be Christians if it weren't for the Christians.

Mahatma Gandhi (1869-1948)

313

If we lived as our enemies live, we would believe what they believe.

Abraham Lincoln (1809-1865)

314

Those who hate you don't win unless you hate them.

Richard Nixon (1913-1994)

315

Education is the process of casting false pearls before real swine.

Irwin Edman

316

Publishing a volume of poetry is like dropping a rose petal down the Grand Canyon and waiting for the echo.

Don Marquis (1878-1937)

317

Sir, there is no settling the point of precedency between a louse and a flea.

Dr Samuel Johnson (1709-1784)

318

'How do you assess the French Revolution?'
'It is a little too early to judge.'

Chou En-Lai (1974)

319

Two Catholic bishops discussing inter-communion:
'At this Conference, I suddenly found non-Catholics coming for communion.'
'What did you do?'
'I didn't know what to do, so I did what Jesus would have done.'
'You didn't!'

320

Why is there only one Monopolies Commission?

321

When they come for the innocent, a curse on you and your religion if they don't have to step over your body.

Philip Berrigan SJ

322

When a man says he is a realist, you can be pretty sure he's about to do something shady.

Isaiah Berlin (b. 1912)

323

God has determined that there be rich people and poor people in the world, so that virtues may be exercised and merits proven.

Pope Pius XI (1939)

324

Education is the transfer of truths from teacher to pupil, without either of them undergoing any change.

325

To claim that everyone should be granted and guaranteed freedom of conscience is one of the most contagious of errors, false and absurd, in fact insane.

Pope Gregory XVI (1832)

326

I have only one little weakness, one secret wish, against which I have long striven in vain – the desire to roast a Quaker.

Sydney Smith (1771-1845)

327

J. B. S. Haldane (1892-1964), being asked what he would conclude about the nature of the Creator from his lifetime study of biology, replied, 'He has an inordinate love of beetles.'

328

'Get off this estate!'
'Why?'
'Because it's mine.'
'How did you get it?'
'From my father.'
'How did *he* get it.'
'From *his* father.'
'And how did *he* get it?'
'He fought for it.'
'Well, I'll fight *you* for it.'

Carl Sandburg (1878-1967)

329

It is as impossible to demonstrate the existence of God as it would be for Sherlock Holmes to demonstrate the existence of Arthur Conan Doyle.

F. Büchner

330

At the very least, prayer is talking to yourself. But that's not a bad idea. Talk to yourself about what matters most, because if you don't, you may forget what matters most.

F. Büchner

331

As the seminary professor lay on his deathbed, his students argued about whether he had already died. 'Feel his feet,' suggested one; 'no one ever died with warm feet.' The professor opened one eye, said, 'Joan of Arc did', and died.

332

'What do you want to be when you grow up?'
'I just want to be alive.'

333

Freedom of worship is the inalienable right of men to worship God according to the teaching of the Catholic church.

1946 statement

334

When Pope Pius IX (1792-1878) was asked for a definition of Tradition, he said 'I am Tradition'.

335

The Bible-translator, John Wyclif, was posthumously condemned in 1415 by the Council of Constance, which ruled that his books be burnt, and that his body be exhumed from his grave in Lutterworth, cremated and thrown into the River Swift.

336

Remember that you are an Englishman, and have consequently won first prize in the lottery of life.

Cecil Rhodes (1853-1902)

337

You become an 'oldie' when your address book contains the names of more dead people than of living ones.

338

Heaven is eating paté de foie gras to the sound of trumpets.

Sydney Smith (1771-1845)

339

The great advantage of not having children must be that you can go on believing that you are a nice person. Once you have children, you realise how wars start.

Fay Weldon

340

What religious abomination do you belong to?

341

If I go as a Hindu, I will meet a Muslim or a Christian.
If I go as a Socialist, I will meet a Capitalist.
If I go as a brown man, I will meet a black man or a white man.
But if I go as a human being, I will meet only human beings.

Satish Kumar

342

The literalist is like someone who goes into a restaurant, sees the word 'steak' on the menu, and eats the card.

Joseph Campbell

343

A fundamentalist is one who obeys the prescription: 'Swallow whole, do not chew.'

Anon

344

'I apologise for cockroaching upon your time.'
'You mean encroaching.'
'No, you are not feminine.'

345

The ultimate tragedy is not the brutality of bad people, but
the silence of good people.

Martin Luther King (1929-1968)

346

The cosmos is a gigantic flywheel making 10,000 revolutions
a minute.
Man is a sick fly taking a dizzy ride on it.
Religion is the theory that the wheel was designed and set
spinning to give him the ride.

Henry L. Mencken (1880-1956)

347

England's greatest problem by far is the servant-problem.
Solve that and everything else falls into place.

Auberon Waugh (b. 1939)

348

One can only admire the majestic impartiality of the law,
which forbids not only the poor, but also the rich, to sleep
rough, beg, or steal bread.

Anatole France (1844-1924)

349

A jury consists of twelve persons chosen to decide which party has a better lawyer.

Robert Frost (1874-1963)

350

The only sure thing about life is that it is unpredictable.

351

You can't shake hands with a fist.

The Dalai Lama (b. 1935)

352

The Prodigal Son took his share of the money, and left home to spend it on rioting, drinking and women. And all the rest he squandered.

353

The aim of the human race is not the survival of the fittest, but the fitting of as many as possible to survive.

Thomas Huxley (1825-1895)

354

God did not simply make all things; he made them make themselves.

Charles Kingsley (1819-1875)

355

I believe in the Holy Catholic Church, and sincerely regret that it does not at present exist.

William Temple (1881-1944)

356

The Church can be the Anti-Christ; and when it denies that possibility, it *is* the Anti-Christ.

Reinhold Niehbur (1892-1971)

357

Nothing can mask the face of God so effectively as religion.

Martin Buber (1878-1965)

358

'Common sense' consists of those prejudices which we acquire before the age of 18.

Albert Einstein (1879-1955)

359

When passenger of foot heave in sight, tootle the horn. Trumpet him melodiously at first, but if he still obstacles your passage, then tootle him with vigour.

Car rental brochure in Tokyo (1993)

360

Those who wed the spirit of the age must expect to find themselves widowed in a very short time.

Dean Inge (1860-1954)

361

Pantheism is a belief in a God who is within all things but not included among them, outside all things but not excluded from them, and above all things but not out of reach.

362

To believe in God is to desire strongly that he exists, and to live as if he does.

363

People are unlovable until you know them.
God is unknowable until you love him.

364

The first thing in life is to assume a pose. What the second one is no one has yet discovered.

Oscar Wilde (1854-1900)

365

He (Tony Benn) is a man who has immatured with age.

Harold Wilson (1916-1995)

366

Fundamentalist Sticker: I Have Found It.
Agnostic Sticker: I'm Still Looking For It.
Jewish Sticker: We Never Lost It.

367

Football is not a matter of life and death: it's far more serious.

Bill Shankly (1913-1981), Manager of Liverpool

368

On the cover of a card: 'Jesus Loves You.'
Inside: 'Everyone else thinks you're a creep.'

369

A future Buddha, seeing a starving beggar, reincarnates as a rabbit and leaps into a fire to make a meal for him – having previously shaken himself three times so that none of the insects in his fur perished with him.

370

'What a class! I've taught you everything I know, and you're still a bunch of idiots.'

371

A Conservative is someone who thinks nothing should ever be done for the first time.

372

Serious sport has nothing to do with fair play. It is bound up with hatred, jealousy, boastfulness and disregard of all rules.

George Orwell (1903-1950)

373

Christianity is not a doctrine, or a theory about what has happened and what will happen to the human soul, but a description of something that actually takes place in human life.

Ludwig Wittgenstein (1889-1951)

374

If babies are innocent, it is not for lack of desire to harm, but only for lack of strength.

St Augustine (354-430) Conf. I,7

375

Roses are red,
Violets are blueish;
If it wasn't for Christmas
We'd all be Jewish.

376

A definition of Evangelism: One beggar telling another where to find bread.

377

I have always said a short prayer to God. Here it is. 'My God, make my enemies completely ridiculous.' God has always granted my request.

Voltaire (1694-1778)

378

When Peter Sellers survived his first heart attack in 1979, Spike Milligan sent him a telegram: 'You swine. I had you insured.'

379

Since I gave up hope I feel much better.

380

We may use animals as we please, as best suits us because they are not humans. Anyone who thinks otherwise is super-stitious and womanish, even (according to Augustine) sinful.

Spinoza (1632-1677)

381

In the US scientists are beginning to use lawyers for their experiments instead of white rats:

1. because there are more lawyers than white rats.
2. because you can't become emotionally attached to a lawyer.
3. because there are some things a white rat just won't do.

382

In the revelation of any truth, there are always three stages. At first it is ridiculed, then it is resisted, and final-ly it is considered self-evident.

383

For a man linked with satire, he (Peter Cook) was without malice to anyone; although he did admit to pursuing an irrational vendetta against the late Gracie Fields.

Richard Ingrams (1995)

384

Here lieth
Goliath.
Nothing stopped him
Till David dropped him.

J. Steig, 'The Old Testament Made Easy'

385

At the Western Wall of the Temple in Jerusalem:
'How often do you come here?'
'Every day I come to pray before these holy stones.'
'And what do you pray for?'
'Peace for Israel, peace for the world.'
'Do your prayers ever get answered?'
'Never. It's like talking to a brick wall.'

386

Some world religions say that people who do not believe in a personal God distinct from themselves are atheists. We Hindus say that a person who does not believe in himself, where the divine splendour dwells, is an atheist.

Swami Vivekananda (1863-1902)

387

If Jesus was Jewish, how come he had a Puerto Rican name?

388

Some Bible Headlines:
JOB: OUTLOOK DISMAL
DAVID 1 : GIANTS 0
LAZARUS OBITUARY: A CORRECTION

389

That denomination is the most prophetic that is willing to die for Christ's sake, to go to its death as deliberately as Christ went to the cross.

P. Ainslie

390

The real atheists are not those who keep asking questions hoping to find a fuller understanding, but those who refuse to ask questions.

391

To say that people should not commit themselves, on the grounds that we live in a pluralist society, is in fact to veto any other commitment than secularism.

392

It is not necessary that the Bible be in the English tongue and in the hands of the common people. The distribution of the Bible, and the permitting or denying it, is totally in the hands of Church authorities.

St Thomas More (1530)

393

The Nicaraguan priest Miguel D'Escoto, suspended in the 1980s by the Vatican (together with the Cardenal priest brothers) for political activity, asked at the age of 63 for the ban to be lifted. He was refused on the grounds that his continued work with the slum dwellers federation proved that he was 'insufficiently repentant'. He has asked that this explanation be buried with him: 'I want to show it to our Lord.'

394

The shortest distance between a human being and the truth is a story.

395

'To become a Teacher of Truth, you must be prepared to be ridiculed, ignored and starving until you are 45.'
'And what will happen when I'm 45?'
'You'll have got used to it.'

Anthony De Mello SJ (1931-1987)

396

Every person is tied to God in heaven by a long string.
Every sin cuts the string, and God has to knot it together again.
The more often you sin, the closer you come to God.

Anthony De Mello SJ (1931-1987)

397

'In the search for God, you must give up all that is dearest to you – wealth, friends, family, country, life itself.'
'And what else?'
'Your beliefs about God.'

Anthony De Mello SJ (1931-1987)

398

In order to reach God, two things are needed:
1. to realise that all efforts to reach God are useless.
2. to act as if you didn't know that.

Anthony De Mello SJ (1931-1987)

399

The Master claimed he had a book telling you everything about God. The student begs to borrow it, excitedly opens it, and finds it blank.
'But the book tells you absolutely nothing!'
'Yes, but what a lot that tells you!'

Anthony De Mello SJ (1931-1987)

400

If you don't want your children to hear what you're saying, pretend you're talking to them.

Miles Kington (b. 1947)

401

A bird in the hand makes it difficult to blow one's nose.

402

In 1939, the archbishop of Canterbury proposed in the House of Lords that all Christians across the world should present a united front against the forces of evil threatening the peace of the world, and that the pope should head this movement. The Catholic Church refused the offer because it might suggest that other Christians were equal to Catholics.

403

Some people see things as they are, and ask 'Why?'
I dream of things that have never been, and ask 'Why not?'

John F. Kennedy (1917-1963)

404

Have Christians subconsciously re-translated the famous text, 'God so loved the world', into 'God so hated the world that he gave his only Son, that whoever does not believe him should perish'?

405

When people ask, 'Where would we be without humour?' I tell them: 'In Germany'.

Willy Rushton (d. 1997)

406

We should pray for the wicked of the world and love them. As long as we don't pray and love in this way, the Messiah can't come.

Sayings of the Rabbis

407

The Emperor Constantine is said to have refused to be baptised until he was on his deathbed. He did not want his sins remitted until he had got them all committed.

408

St Aloysius, patron of purity, is said to have always kept his eyes modestly closed as an infant while he was being suckled at his mother's breast.

409

The saying is that monks ought not to drink wine. But since today no monk believes this, let us at least drink in moderation.

Rule of St Benedict (515)

410

There is at present much dialogue between Catholics and Protestants. But there is really only one important ecumenical question, and it is the deepest – the relationship between Christians and Jews.

Karl Barth (1886-1968)

411

Go and preach the gospel. Use words if necessary.

St Francis of Assisi's advice to his friars (12th century)

412

Ever since they imprisoned him in a Jerusalem storage-well, the Jews have never been able to get Jeremiah out of their cistern.

413

A Dominican, Franciscan and Jesuit were praying together when the lights failed.
The Dominican gave a philosophical lecture on the properties of light.
The Franciscan composed a poem on Sister Light and Brother Darkness.
The Jesuit got up and mended the fuse.

414

If God is, by definition, the ultimate and unknowable mystery, then theology is the only *ology* whose practitioners don't know what they are talking about.

415

We only have Jesus' teaching when he was a young man. That is Christianity. Roman Catholicism is the religion Jesus would have taught if he had lived long enough to be made a cardinal.

Peter De Rosa (b. 1932)

416

Every cleric must obey the pope, even if he commands what is evil: for no one may judge the pope.

Pope Innocent III (1198-1216)

417

To arrive at the truth in all things, we ought always to be ready to believe that what seems to us white is black, if the Church's hierarchy so defines.

St Ignatius Loyola (1491-1556)

418

It is not the least of the troubles of an infallible Church that it cannot decently abandon any position once assumed.

H. C. Lea, 'Studies in Church History' (1883)

419

The Jews have never recognised our Lord. We therefore cannot recognise the Jews.

Pope Pius X (1904)

420

Let no man hold together what God has graciously allowed to fall asunder.

The Bishop of Repton

421

If thy foetus offend thee, pluck it out.

422

Beethoven always sounds to me like the upsetting of a bag of nails, with here and there an also dropped hammer.

John Ruskin (1819-1900)

423

What blows the mind is not the immensity of the star-filled heavens, but the fact that humans have been able to measure them.

Anatole France (1844-1924)

424

How extraordinary that humans who don't know what to do with their lives should want another one which lasts for ever.

Anatole France (1844-1924)

425

When we ask advice, we're usually looking for an accomplice.

Marquis De la Grange (1872)

426

It is easy to get angry: anyone can do it. But to be angry with the right person, to the right extent, at the right time, with the right purpose and in the right way – that is not easy, and not everyone can do it.

Aristotle (BCE 384-322)

427

It is probable that everything is uncertain. But this itself is also quite uncertain.

Pascal (1623-1662)

428

A psychiatrist tells a Jewish mother that her neurotic son is suffering from an Oedipus complex. 'Oedipus schmoedipus', she retorts, 'so long as he loves his mother.'

429

A psychotic is someone who thinks that two and two make five. A neurotic is someone who knows that two and two make four, but just can't stand it.

430

A community which has no synagogue and no shelter for the poor must first provide for the poor.

Jewish teaching (12th century)

431

With the single exception of Homer, there is no eminent writer, not even Sir Walter Scott, whom I can despise so entirely as I despise Shakespeare when I measure my mind against his.

George Bernard Shaw (1856-1950)

432

There are moments when art attains almost to the dignity of manual labour.

Oscar Wilde (1854-1900)

433

To my Eye Rubens's Colouring is most Contemptible. His Shadows are of a Filthy Brown somewhat of the Colour of Excrement.

William Blake (1757-1827)

434

Epitaph for a waiter: By and by, God caught his eye.

Denis McCord

435

Ever since God created humans in his own image, they have been trying to repay the compliment.

Voltaire (1694-1778)

436

If you don't find God in the very next person you meet, it is a waste of time looking any further.

Mahatma Gandhi (1869-1948)

437

Christ has written the promise of resurrection, not in a book, but in every springtime leaf.

Martin Luther (1483-1546)

438

Deep doubts, deep wisdom;
Few doubts, little wisdom.

Chinese proverb

439

Reading poetry in translation is like kissing a woman through a veil.

Chaim Bialik (1873-1934)

440

When you've bought something cheap, you've bought something expensive.

441

The new may be true,
But the old is gold.

442

Those who refuse to make a choice have made a choice.

443

A learned bastard is preferable to an ignorant High Priest.

Midrash on Numbers, Rabbah 6

444

When he asked what was the best way of leading the East Anglians, the new Bishop of Norwich was told: 'Find out which way they're going, and walk in front of them.' *(1992)*

445

The difference between the celibate and the married person is very simply that the celibate denies himself access to two and a half billion women, and the married man to two and a half billion minus one. The difference is not enormous, and should not be exaggerated.

Vatican spokesman (1996)

446

At the end of the tunnel, there is just enough light to show you where the next tunnel begins.

447

Only the shallow know themselves.

Oscar Wilde (1854-1900)

448

He who knows does not speak;
He who speaks does not know.

Lao Tzu (BCE 6th century)

449

Whereof one cannot speak, thereof one must be silent.

Ludwig Wittgenstein (1889-1951)

450

The only thing we can understand about God is that he can't be understood.

St John of Damascus (676-754)

451

The ribs on melons were designed by a wise God so that they can be divided up by a family at table.

Bernadine de St Pierre (1715)

452

I regard religion as a disease born of fear, and as a source of untold misery to the human race.

Bertrand Russell (1872-1970)

453

Anyone who has never been angry against religion has not known too much about it.

454

Anyone who wants to know all about Christianity should read the Sermon on the Mount. Anyone who wants to know even more about Christianity should read the history of its relationship with Judaism.

Rabbi Jonathan Magonet (1975)

455

Nature is as divine a text as the Holy Bible. They can't be in real contradiction with each other.

Galileo (1564-1642)

456

I cannot imagine any omnipotent sentient being suffi-ciently cruel to create the world we inhabit.

Iris Murdoch (b. 1919)

457

Nature, and Nature's laws, lay hid in night;
God said, 'Let Newton be', and all was light.

Alexander Pope (1688-1744)

458

It did not last: the Devil howling, 'Ho!
Let Einstein be!' restored the *status quo*.

Sir John Squire (1920)

459

The philosophers have hitherto only interpreted the world in various ways. The point is, however, to change it.

Inscription on the grave of Karl Marx (1818-1883)

460

Some Jewish schoolchildren passed a dead dog. 'What an awful smell!' said the pupils. 'What magnificent white teeth!' said the teacher.

Bachya (12th century)

461

Those who are not part of the solution are part of the prob-lem.

462

Horse sense is what a horse has that keeps him from betting on people.

W. C. Fields (1879-1946)

463

I don't believe in dying. It's been done.

George Burns (d. 1996)

464

Better keep your mouth shut and be thought a fool, than open it and remove all doubt.

Denis Thatcher

465

Two men on a building site were asked what work they did. One said, 'I'm a bricklayer'. The other said, 'I'm building a cathedral'.

466

'What's Tom's second name?'
'Tom who?'

467

'Why does everyone hate so-and-so at first sight?'
'It saves time.'

468

'The Sermon on the Mount undoubtedly set the highest standard of individual behaviour that anyone could require, but it does not apply to those of us in the House who are responsible for the interests of millions of people.'

An MP in the House of Commons after a US air attack on Libya (April 1986)

469

Life is not one damn thing after another; it is the same damn thing over and over.

470

By all means marry. If you get a good wife you'll become happy. If you get a bad one you'll become a philosopher.

Socrates (BCE 469-399)

471

Those who never make mistakes never make anything.

472

If you love Jesus, you'd better look good on wood.

Dan Berrigan SJ

473

When I pray, I pray quickly because I'm talking to God. But when I read the Bible, I read slowly because God's talking to me.

474

Nothing can be made fool-proof: fools are so ingenious.

475

Hyde Park heckler: 'What shape is the soul?'
Donald Soper (b. 1903): 'Oblong. Next question, please.'

476

Morality is an attitude one adopts towards people one doesn't like.

Oscar Wilde (1854-1900)

477

Aged nun overheard speaking to a statue of St Thérèse: 'And if you had lived as long as me, you wouldn't be a saint either.'

478

The taciturn US President Coolidge (d. 1933) found himself sitting next to a lady at a public dinner, who told him she had made a bet that he would say at least three words to her over the meal. 'You lose', he said, and relapsed into silence.

479

A Catholic bishop asked one of his priests why he had bought a three-quarter size bed. 'Well, I'm half expecting a change.'

480

'A strange horrible business, but good enough I suppose for Shakespeare's day.'

Queen Victoria (1819-1901) on 'King Lear'

481

Concerning God, our safest eloquence is our silence.

Richard Hooker (1554-1600)

482

If we had nothing of the New Testament except the parable of the Prodigal Son, we would have the complete Gospel.

Martin Luther (1483-1546)

483

I sit on a man's back, choking him and making him carry me. And yet I assure myself and others that I am sorry for him, and wish to lighten his load by all possible means – except by getting off his back.

Tolstoy (1882-1945)

484

If there were only one religion in England, there would be danger of tyranny. If there were two, they would cut each other's throats. But since there are thirty, they live happily together in peace.

Voltaire (1694-1778)

485

One almost gets the impression they are being ordained bishops in order to make a public renunciation of humility.

Origen (185-254)

486

How is it that people all manage to die exactly 100 years before their centenary?

487

But if you live the time that no man will give you good
   counsel,
nor no man will give you good example,
when you shall see virtue punished and crime rewarded,
if you will then stand fast and firmly stick to God,
upon pain of my life, though you be but half good,
God will allow you for whole good.

Thomas More (1478-1535)

488

It is only the love which you show them that will make the poor forgive you for the bread you give them.

Vincent de Paul (1581-1660)

489

His conversation never wanes, and it bores.

490

Do not grieve that rosebushes have thorns;
rather rejoice that thornbushes bear roses.

Arab proverb

491

Never tell the truth unless you have one foot in the stirrup.

Arab proverb

492

Our clergy (along with our politicians, police and lawyers) may be deplorable, but they only have the rest of the population to draw on.

493

There are three kinds of country parsons in my diocese. Those who have gone out of their minds. Those who are going out of their minds. And those who have no minds to go out of.

Bishop of Lincoln (1900)

494

I dreamt last night I was in hell, and could not get near the fire for parsons.

Bishop Wilberforce (1850)

495

The Revd Augustus Toplady, author of 'Rock of Ages' (1776) calculated that by the age of thirty, each human being had committed 630,720,000 sins.

496

Continue believing in God, in spite of what the clergy may tell you.

Benjamin Jowett (1817-1893)

497

He cannot have God for his father who refuses to have the Church for his mother.

St Augustine (354-430)

498

The main burden of the sermon was that it was good to be good, but bad to be bad, which while being true and unexceptional, I had previously gathered from other sources.

Bernard Tanner

499

The Revd Frederick Cavell, father of Edith, took literally Paul's advice to Timothy to preach without ceasing, in season and out of season. He preached the same sermon to his congregation every Sunday for 48 years.

500

A sermon is seldom as long as it seems.

Anon

501

If all the people who went to sleep during sermons were laid end to end, they would be far more comfortable.

Anon

502

There is no holy communion without holy community.

John A. T. Robinson (1919-1983)

503

Some ministers would make good martyrs. They are so dry they would burn well.

Charles H. Spurgeon (1834-1892)

504

If God spare my life, ere many years, I will cause a boy that driveth the plough shall know more of the Scripture than thou doest.

William Tyndale (1494-1536)

505

The difference between an organist and a terrorist is that a terrorist can be reasoned with.

506

When the Latin language was dropped for Catholic liturgies, a wise parish priest predicted: 'Be careful. The vernacular in the liturgy will be followed by the perambulator in the presbytery.'

507

An African student coming to study in an English theological college was asked who he was. 'I am a black White Father brother.'

508

Willy Rushton (d. 1997) asked that his tombstone should have only one word: 'Discontinued'.

509

God respects me when I work, but when I sing he loves me.

Rabindranath Tagore (1861-1941)

510

If he died but did not rise,
speak to me not of triumph, but disaster.
If he rose but did not die,
worship with me a ghost, but not my Master.

Peter De Rosa (b. 1932)

511

If I love the world as it is, I am already changing it. A first fragment of the world has been changed, and that is my own heart.

Petru Dumitriu (1964)

512

When I was 17, my father was so stupid he embarrassed me. When I was 21, I was amazed at how much the old man had learned in four years.

Mark Twain (1835-1910)

513

No verbal description of water, however eloquent, will ever be as effective as throwing your pupil into the lake.

Zen saying

514

There are many people who reach their conclusions about life like schoolboys. They cheat their master by copying the answer out of a book, without having worked it out themselves.

Kierkegaard (1813-1855)

515

What God does is best. Probably.

Jewish saying

516

There is no Hebrew or Yiddish word for charity. The word used is *tsedakah*, which means justice.

517

Some Freudian put-downs:
You must come again when you have less time.
Each of his remarks was better than the next.
Is there no beginning to your talents?
Won't anybody put you out of our misery?
You will always have an empty space in my heart.
Nothing is too good for you.

518

When the relics of St Chad (d. 672) were being investigated in Birmingham in 1996, three legs were found instead of the expected two. The archbishop authorised the continuation of devotion to the relics – 'provided that it is directed to all three legs equally'.

Index